ALL THE HOURS

ALL THE HOURS

WILLIAM LYONS

ARCADIA

First published 2022 by
Australian Scholarly Publishing
under its ARCADIA imprint

Australian Scholarly Publishing
7 Lt Lothian St North
North Melbourne, Vic 3051
+63 3 9329 6963
enquiry@scholarly.info
www.scholarly.info

ISBN: 978-1-922669-79-7

Cover: Woodcut – Sean Lingwood, London, 2018
Designer: Amelia Walker

To Adam, Annie, Liz and Margaret

AUTHOR'S NOTE

As the play was being developed, it was submitted as a work in progress to two open-entry, blind-reviewed international play competitions in London for professional feedback. The competition judges had this to say:

> '*An elegant, amusing and entertaining play*' with '*an amusing character in Sister Bernard [depicted] with delightful irreverence*'. The '*witty dialogue engages the reader and some interesting philosophical questions touched me*'.
> — Comments on an early version of the play, under the title 'A Beginning and an End', when it was shortlisted for The Sir Kenneth Branagh Award for New Writing 2017

> '*This play dealt with a sensitive and important issue, and was a compelling read, with a notably charming and engaging protagonist ... an interesting and important piece.*'
> — Comments by the judges of The Papatango New Writing Prize 2017

ACKNOWLEDGEMENTS

I am greatly indebted to Dr Margaret Daly-Denton, a distinguished musician, composer, and scholar of liturgical music, especially of the Liturgy of the Hours, for her advice and warm encouragement throughout the process of writing the play, and to Annie Lyons for so much love for so long. And, of course, to Liz Jones for being so generous as to premiere the play at La Mama and Adam Cass for being so brave as to direct it.

I would also like to acknowledge my use in the play of the *Grail* English translation of the psalms from the Hebrew, in the "inclusive language version" of 1986, but first published by Collins in 1966.

INTRODUCTION
Roma veduta, fede perduta

Those who know me only comparatively recently will wonder how it is that, while being what others would describe as an agnostic in regard to the existence of God, I have written a *simpatico* play about religious belief and "a religious vocation".

It came about like this. I was born into a Catholic family in Melbourne, a family where my close relatives included one bishop, one priest, and sundry nuns. After repeatedly running home at "first break" from the local parish school, I was eventually enrolled at a Jesuit preparatory school Kostka Hall which was near to where we lived in Brighton Beach and, in due course, to its public (i.e. private) secondary school Xavier College, which was not nearby. I was devoutly religious during my schooldays, often rising early during my junior school years to serve at mass in the chapel at Kostka Hall well before classes began. So I decided, on completion of my secondary education, to become a missionary. So, to the chagrin of the Jesuits and astonishment of my family, and perhaps as a sign of embryonic non-conformity, I joined a little known semi-monastic missionary order, called the Missionarii Sacratissimi Cordis (known more simply as the MSCs) and founded by Jules Chevalier in France in the 19TH C. along the lines of a supposed happy mixture of the Benedictines (a monastic religious order) and the Jesuits (a clerks regular religious order). I had changed the uniform of a Catholic boys' school for the uniform of a religious order with no interim period of secular life.

My first year of training as a seminarian, 1958, was spent in spiritual boot-camp called 'a novitiate'. It was located at Douglas Park, New South Wales, away from all distractions in a large rural property that included a farm with cattle, sheep, horses, crops of lucerne, barley, oats and millet, and a dairy. It had once been owned by Sir Thomas Mitchell, a renowned surveyor and explorer of south-eastern Australia who was appointed Surveyor General of New South Wales in 1828. The rather grand sandstone, Gothic revival, colonial mansion built by Mitchell in 1842 was still there and included a fine Anglican chapel and an observation tower. It was named by Mitchell as Parkhall and later by new owners, owing to its nearness to the Nepean River, as Nepean Towers. When the MSCs took possession, they renamed it St Mary's Towers. Douglas Park was also the area where the Dharawal Aboriginal people were systematically all but annihilated by the early settlers and colonial administrators.

We new recruits to the religious life were called novices and the priest in charge the Novice Master. The Novice Master was a thin and ascetic man who wore spectacles. When he walked about, he kept his head bent forward and his eyes on the ground, practising that "custody of the eyes" which we were told was essential to avoiding temptation, particularly the temptations of the flesh incited by seeing a female of almost any age or status. The Novice Master seemed very rarely to permit a smile to animate his features. I recall that one day when he was instructing us in the spiritual life, he discussed the life of the 16TH C Spanish mystic, John of Avila, remarking with approval that it was said of him that "he never had a joke in his mouth". His day seemed to be divided between teaching and supervising us, saying mass, reading and praying in his small room, and meditating in the chapel. However, to his credit, I did not get the impression that he took pleasure in the many hard things he had to do and say to us over the year of our novitiate.

Like army recruits, on arrival we were given a haircut and each morning a cold shower whatever the season, and issued with a worn or patched version of our religious uniform as well as the Constitution of the order. Our uniform was a black religious habit secured around the waist with a black woollen cord, black trousers and socks, and an ecclesiastical "dog collar" attached to a black bib. The novices' day was strictly ordered. We rose at five in the morning, showered, dressed, and then went to morning prayers in the chapel followed by an hour of meditation on some pre-arranged passage from scripture or other approved spiritual writings. Then to breakfast in silence. Until lunch we had classes about the religious life conducted entirely by the Novice Master. Many of these were centred on passages in the Constitution of the order but others were on passages from religious authors about the religious life. Sometimes these classes took the form of the Novice Master listing our faults (names attached) in public – being late for something, breaking the rule of silence, being slovenly, and so on. Lunch was taken in silence while one of the novices read from some edifying text at a lectern. Then in the afternoon we engaged in manual work, sometimes on the farm or, on Wednesdays I think it was, and Sundays, we were permitted to go for a walk. Our favourite destination was a stretch of the Nepean River where, in summer, we might go swimming. One afternoon on our walk to the swimming hole I saw my first goanna that was not in a zoo.

During these recreational afternoons we were permitted to converse. After returning and showering we engaged in spiritual reading in chapel, followed by supper, night prayers, a short period of recreation and conversation, then bed at nine o'clock. The length of all meals was governed by the Novice Master's saying grace to begin and ringing a bell to end a meal, followed by a closing grace. Often, it seemed to me, the Novice Master deliberately rang the bell while most of us were still eating. This, I presumed, was one of his many lessons for us about learning to do "the hard thing" and forego "the easy thing" and so about how to arm ourselves against the self-serving ego which is the enemy of morality. I fear that I have too often failed to learn from these lessons.

Not long after our arrival we were issued with "the discipline" which was a whip made of thin slips of leather, knotted at intervals and gathered into a grip at one end. We had to use this to scourge our naked backs every Friday morning, the day of the week of Christ's death according to ecclesiastical tradition, when the bell rang at five o'clock and for the duration of a silently and unhurriedly recited Lord's Prayer. This imposition was to remind us of Christ's suffering as well as to teach us in another way to do "the hard thing" which in turn would prepare us to resist especially the temptation to succumb to "the sins of the flesh" during our later religious life. While I dutifully performed this self-harming ritual over my six years as a seminarian, I always found it difficult and could never sleep well on a Thursday evening. Particularly distressing during my novitiate was the sound of these commingled self-beatings assaulting the Friday morning silence in our thinly-partitioned dormitory. Perhaps becoming an apprentice flagellant did me some good. I do not know.

The novitiate ended with our being measured and then provided with new tailored versions of the MSC religious uniform. These habits were made on the premises by a small number of the religious brothers in the order whose daily work was tailoring. Then, neat and smart in our new habits, and in the presence of our parents, we took our solemn religious vows of poverty, chastity and obedience in the chapel. We were now full members of our order, the Missionaries of the Sacred Heart, and destined eventually after many further years of study and training to become priests, most of whom would teach in some missionary field in Oceania or in an Australian school run by the order. The religious brothers on the other hand remained for the rest of their life as they were, brothers engaged mainly in manual labour.

Immediately after the novitiate year, I was sent for a year to the MSC monastery at Croydon in Victoria. Though I recall little of the curriculum, I remember attending some classes in philosophy and recall a visit from the distinguished Australian philosopher and public intellectual, Max Charlesworth, who, in a series of talks based on his first book *Philosophy and Linguistic Analysis*, introduced us to some aspects of modern Anglophone analytic philosophy. Another part of the curriculum was an introduction to Biblical Hebrew. The language was very different in structure from the classical Latin and Attic Greek that I had studied at school. Its alphabet was made up of calligraphic block script and its texts seemed to be full of consonants with no vowels. The latter having to be added later by means of dots and other marks so that the words could be correctly pronounced out loud during religious services. A Hebrew text was also read from right to left. We learnt too that *Yahweh* both is and is not the word for God. Sadly this introductory course, so fascinating, was not added to in the later years of my training and I've never got around to adding to it.

The next part of my training as a seminarian, took me to the newly built MSC house in Canberra to study mainly Thomistic philosophy (the Aristotelian philosophy underlying the theology of St Thomas Aquinas and modified by him) and ecclesiastical history. It was located on the Federal Highway, at that time still "in the bush" but by now a built-up suburban area. By a great stroke of luck, as part of their education for me, they sent me to study classics at the Australian National University (for I had studied Latin and Greek, as well as mathematics, physics and chemistry, throughout secondary school – my father did not believe in the separation of C. P. Snow's "two cultures"). The Head of Classics at ANU's School of General Studies at that time was K. C. Masterman. To the amusement of his students, we learnt that the 'C' stood for Chauncey, which sounded to us like the name of an aristocratic character in a comedy by Oscar Wilde or Edwardian-style comic novel by P. G. Wodehouse. In fact he was a very tweedy English gentleman with impeccable social graces, a very posh accent, and an agreeably dry academic wit. He was also a very good scholar and teacher.

By an even greater stroke of good fortune, while I was "majoring" in classics, as part of the degree requirements I had to take some "minors". So I attended lectures in English and Philosophy. The philosophy lectures I remember best from that period, and they were excellent, were those given by Kurt Baier and Ray Bradley. Kurt Baier, at that time Head of the Philosophy Department, was one of the "Dunera Boys" who had escaped from Nazi Germany but, via internment in England as an alien, had then been transported to Australia in the HMT Dunera and placed in prison camps. The "Dunera Boys" later contributed so much to the cultural life of Australia. Ray Bradley was a young, enthralling and provocative undergraduate lecturer. I became "hooked" on philosophy.

After two years as an undergraduate in classics at the ANU, the MSCs sent me to study theology at the Gregorian University in Rome. My classics background proved useful as the *lingua franca* of "The Greg" was Latin. But not enormously useful as the Jesuit professors, who lectured us at "The Greg", spoke a bastardized version of medieval Latin with a German or French or Spanish or American accent. So I also found myself having to speak in Latin from time to time – may Cicero and Livy forgive me. More crucially the contrast between being lectured at "The Greg" in mediaeval Latin, examined orally in Latin in a "what you can regurgitate by rote" atmosphere, with the instruction involving no essays, no discussion, and no "feed-back" of any sort, and the "open society" at the ANU, especially in philosophy, proved unsettling.

However, living in a seminarian student house in the Aventine hills of Rome – the house is now a private secondary school for the children of the well-to-do – and travelling on foot to the university every day past the Circus Maximus, Palatine Hill, Forum and Colosseum was an education in classical history and architecture of a rare immediacy. I can still conjure up the images of these places from memory, the traces gladly strengthened by some later "laicised" visits to Rome.

Another unsettling matter was that, a year and a half after I arrived in Rome, having recently taken "minor orders" (porter, lector, cantor, exorcist and acolyte), I was told to think seriously about "the next step", namely the taking of "major orders" (sub-diaconate, diaconate, and then priesthood). I did take it very seriously and, after many sleepless nights and troubled days while "on retreat", I handed in my notice to the gentle and lugubrious French priest who ruled over our student residence as abbot. Upon serious reflection, I had decided that I was not really suited to the clerical life and a fortiori to a semi-monastic version of it. In part I blame the women of Rome, the mere sight of them, for my defection – clearly a failure on my part in regard to "custody of the eyes". As the local proverb has it, *Roma veduta, fede perduta.* But these years with the MSCs were definitely not wasted. In particular I am forever grateful for the austere lessons in psychological self-sufficiency and the habits of studiousness. I was also the recipient of great and continual kindness, and of genuine friendship. The order had, in addition, clothed, fed, housed and educated me for six years. I am still in their debt.

Though I've always thought of music as the greatest of the arts, I have sadly to admit that my time in the ecclesiastical cloisters made it clear to me that I'm part of that lumpen audience that cannot "hear" music so as to hold a tune properly, but must respond to music mainly through the emotions. My singing ability was so risible when I was a seminarian that, even though the musical task might be to sing a simple line of Gregorian chant, the Kapellmeister often felt compelled to ask me to refrain from singing and to lip sync. But this does not stop me from listening to music and enjoying it in an unsophisticated way.

At any rate, after returning from Rome rather shamefacedly to face my devoutly religious family in Australia, I asked my parents if I could resume my undergraduate studies at the ANU, rather than live at home and go to Melbourne University. I was by now 24 years of age, and had been awarded a Commonwealth Scholarship (on the basis of my school matriculation results). While still a "remittance man", I was edging towards financial independence, and so my parents, somewhat reluctantly, agreed. When I re-enrolled at the ANU, I enrolled as a "major" in philosophy. Because of my change of major subject, I was told that I would have to do another three years of undergraduate study on top of the two I had already done. As this would involve only the study of philosophy, I was delighted rather than put out. After a year of study, or was it two, when my Commonwealth Scholarship ran out, I was awarded an ANU Scholarship (on the basis of my record at the ANU up to that point), though I recall that the generous flow of "maintenance money" from my parents did not cease.

First gradually during those years of philosophy at the ANU, then more swiftly and completely during the following *lustrum*, my belief in the tenets of Catholicism gradually drained away. I am no longer religious in the sense that I am no longer a member of any religion. I have no good arguments to demonstrate that God does not exist but equally no good arguments that lead me to believe God does exist. My mind lies in the in-between. Yet I am still moved by the choral masterpieces of religious worship and always humbled by the labour and devotion and skill that went into the creation of the artistic magnificence of the great cathedrals of Christendom, temples of Judaism and mosques of Islam. So I am, I suppose, aesthetically religious.

But in the final analysis I believe mainly in some great cosmic source of energy and matter, some Awesome IT, that began its work with the Big Bang. I cannot but marvel at the scale and power of IT's myriad worlds that cosmology and astrophysics are gradually revealing to us. This Awesome IT reveals itself, in so far as it does, as not being a personal god of any sort, male or female or rainbow, and so as not being someone who gives a damn about us humans. It appears to be just a great impersonal force. It seems that eventually we must all reluctantly admit that our world is just one among many and our solar system one among many and our cosmos one among many. Furthermore in the long history of our planet we humans are Johnny-Come-Latelies with no special status, except what we have awarded ourselves through our imagination and vanity. In cosmic panorama we are simply a recently added pixel in the background. Yet, for me, there is something quasi-religious in realizing and then accepting this.

I come to this view somewhat regretfully, as it would be much more comforting, being now in old age and beset with its usual indignities and infirmities, to believe in a personal God who perhaps will show me mercy before His tribunal and then lead me gently into a suite in His Heavenly Eventide Home. I sometimes imagine myself at this tribunal pleading that, religiously speaking, since I was a seminarian for six years, I had done my National Service. Thus, and ever more frequently as I near personal extinction, I envy those who have the solace of genuine religious belief and I would certainly never have any interest in trying to undermine or alter their beliefs in any way. After all they may simply be right and me wrong.

ALL THE HOURS

Dramatis Personae

Sister Bernard   A Cistercian nun of "strict observance" aged in her late sixties, dressed in the Cistercian working dress of black veil, white robe and black scapular, brown leather belt, black stockings and shoes.

Chorus of Nuns   Four Cistercian nuns who sing the Hours a cappella. They are dressed in the more formal Cistercian dress of black veil, with the white choir cawl which completely covers the robe and scapular.
[If the production budget is constrained, the a cappella chanting of the psalms could be pre-recorded.]

Reverend Mother Albert   The Abbess of the Cistercian Abbey – she appears only very briefly at the very end of the play. She is dressed in the Cistercian working dress of black veil, white robe and black scapular, brown leather belt black stockings and shoes.

The scene, for the whole play, is just one room, the convent cell of Sister Bernard, a Cistercian nun. In the cell is a bed with a crucifix above it, a chamber-pot under the bed, a plain table on which there is an electric desk-light, some books, a large lined notebook cum diary, and a pen, then a chair and a plain oak prie-dieu.

VIGILS

It is midnight and **Sister Bernard** *is* **in bed** *in her "regulation" plain white nun's nightgown.* **The abbey bell sounds** *calling the nuns to chant* **Vigils** *– namely the psalms and antiphons that herald the beginning of the new round of liturgical hours.*

Sister Bernard   *(After* **rising from bed** *at the sound of the bell, she* **takes the chamber-pot** *from under the plain pallet bed, lifts up her nightdress and sits on it.)*

I'm sure dear Aunty Bridget thought nuns didn't have bodily functions. Or, if they did, they'd be some sort of Immaculate Evacuation.

(After a moment or two she **gets up, puts the chamber-pot back under the bed,** *and quickly* **dons her religious habit, shoes etc.** *in silence.)*

Chorus of Nuns   *(Beginning the chant. As soon as the chanting starts, **Sister Bernard kneels** at the prie-dieu, facing the audience, and listens to the chanting of Psalm 5.)*

To my words give ear, O lord,
Give heed to my groaning.
Attend to the sound of my cries,
My king and my God.

It is you whom I invoke, O Lord,
In the morning you hear me;
In the morning I offer you my prayer,
Watching and waiting.

Lead me, Lord, in your justice,
Because of those who lie in wait;
Make clear your way before me.

*(**Sister Bernard joins in the chant** when the last two lines are repeated.)*

Because of those who lie in wait
Make clear your way before me.

Sister Bernard   *After the chanting has finished, she stands up.)*

Why they sing of morning, beats me.

Vigils's midnight!

Even the birds don't sing at this hour.

Except the owl who thinks it's all a bit of a
hoot.

Sorry, sorry. I'm not at my best at this hour.

But I like singing, and Saint Augustine did
say "To sing is to pray twice".

Though he might have revised that if he had
to stand next to Sister Patrick in choir.

Well, as I said, it's now midnight. With me
going back to bed afterwards for a good
bout of tossing and turning until daytime.

'Bout' is right. Sometimes, at the sound of
the bell, I feel like a boxer coming out of
his corner, with me way behind on points.

Way behind.

That's why I'm here, confined to my cell;
not with the others in choir.

Doing penance.

'Cos of what I said to Dom Boniface when
he came to give us our annual retreat.

I call him Ol' Boneyface, by the way, but

not to his face, of course. You don't get to speak to him anyway.

(Starts to walk about around her cell, ruminating.)

We Cistercian nuns don't get to do a lot of speaking, full stop.
Rule of silence.
I can talk to myself. Or to God.
That doesn't count.
Unless it's too loud and might annoy Sister Patrick next door.
But she's pretty deaf nowadays. And there's no one on the other side.
My cell is "end of terrace".

(Stops walking.)

But, as I was saying, I call him Ol' Boneyface because he's like a walking cadaver. And, like Saint John of Avila, never had a joke in his mouth.

Anyway it was like this. Ol' Boneyface was going on in his homily about how we women were the Church's handmaidens

and one of our joyous duties was to help
God's priests by making vestments and
communion wafers and all that stuff.
I must have been having another bad day,
as I shouted out, real loud, "I thought we
were bloody brides of *Christ*? Not clerics'
house-keepers!"

Ol' Boneyface lost track, mumbled
something and strode out.
Furiously.
He must have gone straight to Reverend
Mother after choir and complained.

(*Starts to walk around her cell once again.*)

I know, I know. I'm a nun. A sort of *über-*
nun, a Cistercian of Strict Observance.
Shut away and silent, with prayer my main
duty.
So, right, I shouldn't have said that to Ol'
Boneyface.
I shouldn't have said anything. I should be
ashamed.

But I'm not. It's a convent.

A place for nuns. Women.
Yet the whole show is still... so male.

To give you the flavour. My name's
Sister Bernard. *Bernard*!
Bernard's a boy's name, right?
Why not, say,... Clotilde or Martha
or Melina?

I suppose Clotilde would be out because
she was a married saint. And probably
enjoyed a bit of... yer know, yer know.

Well then what about Hildegard?
Hildegard von Bingen was classy.
An abbess, composer, poet, visionary ...
Wow! Heavyweight champion. And no
time for any "yer know, yer know".

Okay, okay. I enjoyed boxing. I used to
watch it on the box with me Dad.
He'd been a good amateur. Middleweight.

He'd watch a fight on the Tele and after one
round tell you who was going to win.
Rarely wrong. He'd say things like,
"See that flashy feller in the purple trunks?

Doesn't have any weight in his punches.
About round three the other feller will
come inside and put a big one on him".
Or "Look at that heavyweight. All the
weight in the wrong place. A punch to his
paunch will crumple him up".

(Stops walking.)

Anyway, next day, I was summoned to see
Reverend Mother Abbess, *subito*, to
explain my rudeness to Dom Boneyface.

Tell you the truth, I copped out.
Vow of obedience, you see.
I just double-zipped my mouth and listened
to how it was not merely rude of me,
'insolent' was the word she used, but an
insult to holy Father Boniface, to the Order,
the Pope, the Church and... probably all
the Cherubim and Seraphim as well.

I heard her but didn't listen.
I just tuned out, dreaming of spaghetti and
meat-balls.
When she'd finished, I just said I was sorry.

The upshot was I'm "confined to my cell",
until she, that's Reverend Mother Albert
— yeah, hey, hey, hey, a boy's name again,
like Sister Patrick next door — until she
thinks I've become a good girl again.
Funny isn't it how I slip into using the
words 'boy' and 'girl', not 'man' and
'woman'. Where are you, Dr Freud?

(She sits down on the edge of her bed and puts her head in her hands.)

LAUDS

*It is three o'clock in the morning and **Sister Bernard** is **napping on her bed** with her clothes on, except for her shoes which are beside the bed. **The abbey bell sounds** calling the nuns to chant the "hour" of Lauds – namely the psalms and antiphons that remind the nuns of their duty to praise the Lord and seek his help.*

Sister Bernard   *(At the sound of the bell, she arises from the bed.)*

You're wondering what I've been doing
back in bed again.
You think I'm some sort of recidivist.
But unless I have a nap after Vigils,

with a resurrection at Lauds,
I'd never make it to Compline.

I suspect we all do it, except perhaps
Reverend Mother who's some sort of long-
distance austerity champion.

It's just three o'clock in the morning and
that was the bell for Lauds. So it's Praise
the Lord in the wee hours' time.

Chorus of Nuns *(As soon as the chanting starts,*
Sister Bernard moves away from the bed
*and once again **kneels** at the prie-dieu,*
facing the audience, at the left-hand side of
the stage and listens to the chanting of
Psalm 61.)

O god, hear my cry!
Listen to my prayer!
From the end of the earth, I call;
My heart is faint.

Let me dwell in your tent for ever
And hide in the shelter of your wings.
For you, O god, hear my prayer,

Grant me the heritage of those who fear you.

So I will always praise your name
And day after day fulfill my vows.

(Sister Bernard joins in the chant when the last two lines are repeated.)

So I will always praise your name
And day after day fulfill my vows.

Sister Bernard   *(After the chanting has finished, she stands up.)*

Vows, vows, rules, regulations, sacrifice.
Holy BDSM.

(Then she goes to the table and sits down at it. She then takes up one of the four books stacked on the table.)

I'm not allowed more than four books at a time in my cell.
Even when I'm doing "solitary".
Approved books. Improving books.
There are some books in the library you've

got to ask Reverend Mother's permission to read.
A book, say by James Joyce, wouldn't even be in the library.

At any rate, she chose four books for me to be read during my penance.
"Slow movers" all of them.Costive stuff.
So no risk I'd finish them in a hurry.
I noticed that the top one was *The Letters of Hildegard of Bingen*, with a slip of paper marking page 72 and the penciled message "read half way down".

(Picking up this book.)

I think this is the bit she means. Hildegard is writing to the Abbess of Bamberg, in about the year 1158:
"Therefore you should restrain and discipline your daughters (meaning the nuns in her convent) in all matters".

So, I guess, that's Reverend Mother Albert waiving the rod at me, one of her wayward daughters.

Mother, daughter. One big happy family.

Though the family is getting smaller.
No postulants again this year. An almost extinct species.
The last of the holy Mohicans.

Reverend Mother also told me to keep a spiritual diary during my penance. To help me concentrate.
I'm not sure how long it will last, by the way. This penance.
She just said "until God's grace has had time to cure your wickedness".
Well I'll do the diary bit, but I'm not sure how well the spiritual bit will go.
But here goes.

*(Still sitting down at the plain table, she **begins to write** in a large lined notebook, pausing every now and again to ponder.)*

Yesterday I was reading again in *The Letters of Hildegard of Bingen*. A favourite of Reverend Mother Albert.
Maybe a bit of snobbery there.

Hildegard was an aristocrat and a regular correspondent of popes, bishops and abbesses.

I can't honestly say I'm a Hildegard fan.
Her mysticism and visions keep me at a distance.
She's the one at the party who stands by herself in the corner sniffing a flute of chilled Sancerre while the rest of us drink beer from cans in the middle of the noisy room.
And *we* never get to smell or even see the Sancerre, much less taste it.
We just hear about it, afterwards, from her.

And there's no denying there's a bit of envy here.
With us ordinary nuns, God's secretary says "Thanks for the prayers. Call us again on the answer-phone anytime".
For her it's "No need to call, we'll call you".

(Pondering, and not writing.)

I didn't get to confession last week because

I was confined here in my cell,
"doing penance".
We nuns go to confession in the marvelous
Gothic confection in our abbey church.
It's built of carved oak,
like a cathedral in miniature.
Fr Benedict sits in the middle cubicle.
On either side of him are curtained cubicles
with a slide. After he's finished hearing the
confession of someone in the cubicle on the
other side, Fr Benedict opens the slide on
my side, though it's only to allow him to
hear me.
He can't really see me or touch me, as the
slide has a metal grille as well as a curtain.

I have to go to confession once a week,
whether I want to or not.
But what can I get up to here?
In an enclosed convent?
No great opportunities for sinning.
What could I do that'd get me into
purgatory, much less into hell?

(Stands up and walks about.)

But I always try to think of something, so Father Benedict won't feel he's wasting his time.

I say things like, "I'm very impatient, particularly with poor old Sister Dalmatia". I've no excuse for my sharp intakes of breath and occasional expletive when she wanders into the kitchen where we're working and knocks things over.

I'm pretty sure Dalmatia has the beginnings of Alzheimer's. Or more than the beginnings. I should be kinder to her.

Her religious name, Dalmatia, doesn't help. It makes me think of her as a rather goofy old spotted dog. In fact the original Saint Dalmatia was a Syrian hermit of long ago. Sort of appropriate for this place.

OK, I also "touch myself" now and again, and so I tell Fr Benedict about it. But I can't see the wrong in this. It's my finger and my vagina. Who's being harmed? Certainly not me.

God wouldn't like it, Fr Benedict would say.
But he's not getting it, I'd like to reply.
But I don't, of course.

What really happens is that I get a long
sermon from Fr Benedict on my body being
really God's vessel and its just being on loan
to me, for He made everything. I'm
accused, you might say, of having my
fingers in God's till.

I once replied, after he'd wound down a bit,
that I thought our lives were *dona dei*, gifts
from God, and so we should be able to do
what we like with them, given we cause no
harm to anyone.
Wasn't it a package deal, with "free will"
the ribbons on top?

Who gives a gift and then says "Here's the
book of rules about what you can and
cannot do with this gift"?
But Fr Benedict said my being cheeky to him
just made matters worse.

(Sings.)

So I will always praise your name
And day after day fulfill my vows.

So many vows.
So many promises.
Promises, promises.

Telling Fr Benedict about my two-finger
fugue reminded me of my childhood.
I once told my brother Tom, who was
much younger than me, that his penis
was called "a winky". With ignorant
prescience, he then christened my vagina
a "wanky".
So was born that famed international
double act,
"Winky and Wanky".
Such pre-apple innocence.

I also have less than "holy holy" thoughts.
I own up.
Sometimes I have real, grade A, lascivious
ones.
Some recently about that young Polish
monk who came to say mass for us.
I imagine him taking me from behind.

In technicolour. Really letting myself go.

And him too.

Dog and bitch.

OK, OK. That's terrible. Appalling.

Sacrilegious.

A holy nun talking like a guttersnipe.

Becoming like an animal, Fr Benedict said,

when I told him. But I said, we are animals.

Bipedal primates with opposable thumbs.

Cousins of the great apes.

By this time Fr Benedict was sweating,

getting very angry and his voice becoming

quite shaky. So he piled on the penance.

I like that "Pile on the penance". It would

have made a good pop song sung by the

gravelly-voiced Bob Dylan, with his

harmonica wailing alongside.

*(In a Bob Dylan-like voice, she **sings**.)*

Pile on the penance, Sister Sin,

Till your knees are red and raw.

Pile on the penance, Sister Sin,

Till your soul is sorry and sore.

Pile on the penance...Pile on...

*(Here her voice trails away. She leans back
and says.)*

Sometimes Fr Benedict's penance was penal,
and really hurt. After telling him about
one of my more lascivious daydreams, he
handed me a holy scourge through the little
trapdoor in the confessional. It was made
of knotted leather and, with its own
definite article, called "The Discipline".
Thus it was I became an apprentice
flagellant and beat my bare back each
morning for a week.
The length of time was my reciting
The Lord's Prayer.
I often hurried.

But I sort of like old Fr Benedict and so,
when I see him angry and squirming, I do
feel sorry for him.
It can't be much fun listening to the sad and
shriveled sins of enclosed-order nuns.

The convent confessors like Fr Benedict are

all old, you see, so they're no longer
supposed to be troubled by "sins of th
flesh".
Fr Benedict usually smells of cheap whisky.
The sort of stuff my Dad called "Panther's
Piss".
GLEN something-or-other or VAT
something-or-other.
Fr Benedict's way of getting through the
dark hours; drowning his loneliness.

At least I've never heard he's one of those
who fiddle with little boys' diddles.
What an appalling crime against the
innocent that is.
By men who don the uniform of sanctity.
Paedophile suits.
Suffer little children…
It's like a policeman being outed as a drug
dealer, or a philosopher selling his mind to
some murderous ideology for preferment.
Trahison des clercs.

*(**Standing up** from her table and **stretching**.
Then **sits down again and returns to***

writing in her diary.)

I wonder what sins Fr Benedict confesses?
Perhaps he says, "When I hear Sister
Bernard's confession, I pretend I'm deafer
than I am and get her to repeat the rude
bits".

He's just God's ear trumpet after all.
God Himself wouldn't blush of course.
He's heard everything before.

I suspect Fr Benedict was one of those who
were more or less priests in junior school,
graduating from some sort of junior
seminary school into a monastery,
without ever having lived in "the real
world", as they say.

At least I was in "the real world" for some
twenty years and a bit. It was gaining a
distaste for much of it that led me into this
place.
Swopping "the real world" for a very unreal
one, one of my brothers said.
An escape? I hope not. But maybe.

Who knows. Too late now.
I wouldn't survive anywhere else.

If Reverend Mother ever gets to read this
diary, it will be consigned immediately to
her *opera damnata* cupboard. With its
double lock.
Good company though.
Descartes, Hobbes, Locke, Voltaire, Hume,
Kant, Bentham…
Most of the books on my undergraduate
philosophy reading list are there.

PRIME

*It is now six o'clock in the morning and **Sister Bernard** is
dressed and **pacing the floor**. **The abbey bell sounds** calling
the nuns to chant their Prime prayers – namely the psalms
and antiphons that remind the nuns of their duty to herald
with prayer the first hour of the new God-given day.*

*At the sound of the bell, **Sister Bernard** once again **kneels at
the prie-dieu** and awaits the chanting of Psalm 137.*

Chorus of Nuns   *(Chanting.)*

By the rivers of Babylon
There we sat and wept,

Remembering Zion;
On the poplars that grew there
We hung up our harps.

For it was there that they asked us,
Our captors, for songs.
Our oppressors, for joy.
"Sing to us," they said,
One of Zion's song."

O let my tongue
Cleave to my mouth
If I remember you not,
If I prize not Jerusalem
Above all other joys!

(Sister Bernard as usual joins in the chant
when the last two lines are repeated.)

If I prize not Jerusalem
Above all other joys!

Sister Bernard   *(After the chanting has finished, she stands*
up and starts to pace the floor again.)

Jerusalem. A convent?
Can that be what was meant?

*(Continues pacing until **the door of her cell is opened a fraction** and a plate of porridge, a glass of water and a spoon are pushed around the door. She **picks up the dish and glass and puts them on her table, sits down and begins to eat.**)*

Porridge. It's almost always porridge for breakfast.
Including feast days, when you get porridge with a dollop of honey on it and milk instead of water.

*(**Takes a mouthful** and makes a face, of disgust.)*

Swallow, not savour.
The Norwegians call porridge Grøt!
Sounds just about right.

*(After a **couple more mouthfuls.**)*

Perhaps porridge for breakfast strikes the right note.
After all I'm "doing porridge", aren't I, for my Boneyface sins?

*(Some **more mouthfuls.**)*

And who am I to complain about porridge
for breakfast?
When Wittgenstein visited his Irish friend,
Con Drury, he warned him he didn't want
any fancy food.
Said he wanted the same menu every day –
porridge for breakfast, vegetables for lunch,
and a boiled egg in the evening.
He'd love it here!

*(Another **mouthful.**)*

Though, on second thoughts, he might not.
I seem to recall that Wittgenstein wasn't too
comfortable with women.

*(Another **mouthful.**)*

Besides he'd drive Reverend Mother around
the bend, suggesting how to improve the
vegetable garden, criticize the chapel
architecture, and want to sack most of the
choir.

*(After a **final couple of mouthfuls** and a*

swig of water.)

But then porridge didn't seem to do him any harm.

So, dear Porridge, may your honest *sonsie* face enlighten my mind, even as you weigh down my stomach!

*(She **drinks more water**. The she **gets up and starts to pace** the floor again, fairly quickly this time.)*

I need to work off the porridge for a bit.

Though lately I've wondered about my pacing around my cell so much.

As a teenager I used to watch the poor old polar bear, at the zoo, pacing first two steps to the right, then two to the left, then the same again almost endlessly.

A two-step of despair.

His forlorn fret for freedom.

*(Pauses but then **continues pacing. Then stops**.)*

Our monastic enclosure is meant to be an aid to contemplation. A way of blocking out the distractions of the world.

Freeing us *from* the world.

In solitary silence one is said to hear better

the voice of God.

That's what the theologians say.

If only I had the faith of dear old

Sister Teresa.

She lives with her gaze upwards, constantly

communing with God.

She couldn't live in the world anyway.

The world couldn't live with her.

She'd wander into the traffic, with her gaze

heavenwards, blind to the chaos all round.

She'd forget to eat.

I suspect she'd like to be a pure soul,

floating around,

not weighed down by a body.

A Bodhisattva in a black scapula.

(Begins again to pace.)

Sadly, I'm no Sister Teresa.

I was in the world too long.

I enjoyed the world.

Perhaps too much.

Now after all these years I still struggle to forget it.

I loved good food, friendship. Wine.
Intimacy.
Dear Lord, there's nothing like the intimacies of lovers. They can do anything they like. "Your desire is my desire".
Humani nihil a me alienum puto.

*(Pause, **standing still**.)*

Of course, when there isn't love, intimacy is harassment or assault or invasion.
Or just a bore.

Dear Lord, now and again I'd love a bit of invasion.
But it's *noli me tangere* in the monastic life.
Much harder on women.

OK Father Benedict, I'll confess all this next time round. And you can break out into a sweat again and lay on the heavy penance.
(In mock Shakespearian voice.)
Lay on MacBenedict and damned be him who cries, Hold enough!

(Begins pacing again.)

But it's really just a cliche´, isn't it, to say
nuns are women who have been
disappointed in love?

Certainly I loved Charlie, though my
mother didn't.
"Don't trust a man who parts his hair in
the middle", she'd say.
We were together for six years,
Charlie and I.
Then he went off with Fiona Fat Thighs.
She was posh. Pots of money.

It's easier for men. They seem to be able to
pull the birds more or less at any age.
And then push them away again. Always
wanting new season's spring lamb.

Our biological clock doesn't help. Gives us
a sell-by date.
Men don't seem to have one.
And they always see themselves as the
captain of the ship, even when they
couldn't steer a paddle-boat in a pond.

When men get bored with playing with women, they play their *other* game. Dress up in uniforms, fire at one another, award themselves medals, and then forget about those who've lost their legs or lives.

Yeah, I know. Christ was a man.
An unorthodox Jewish student who said turn the other cheek. No swords or spears.
No "eye for an eye", no *lex talionis*.

But then the Romans fixed him, didn't they.
They took playing soldiers *very* seriously.

(Pause.)

Did St Benedict get it wrong then?
Enticing us out of the world, to hide us away?
Away from the divine grandeur of the world.
Why isn't that a sin?
We're warned about the unexamined life.
But what about the unlived life?

*(Pause, then **starts pacing again**.)*

Perhaps St Benedict's telling me I should
be trying to prise open the door into
another and better and higher world.

But that's like offering heavenly life for our
tired-out tradesman's entrance one.
Not an appeal to our finest motives, is it.
If we last the course, will it be seventy
virgins for the monks, and six-pack surfers
for the nuns?

OK, Fr Benedict, sorry for the doubts.
But what is faith without doubts? Dressing
up in a uniform, marching about and
saluting, but never engaging in combat?
The devil and his apple again.
Should I look to see if I have a devil's
nipple?

*(Sister Bernard starts her **pacing once
again**.)*

TERCE

*It is now nine o'clock in the morning and **Sister Bernard** is
dressed and seated at her table, writing in her diary. **The
abbey bell sounds** calling the nuns to chant their Terce*

prayers – namely the first of the three "hours" whose psalms and antiphons commemorate the passion of Christ and commend to the nuns the sacred labours of the day.

At the sound of the bell, Sister Bernard stands up, moves away from her table *and once again* **kneels at the prie-dieu,** *awaiting the chanting of Psalm 23.*

Chorus of Nuns   *(Chanting.)*

> The Lord is my shepherd;
> There is nothing I shall want.
> Fresh and green are the pastures
> Where he gives me repose.
>
> Near restful waters he leads me,
> To revive my drooping spirit.
> He guides me along the right path;
> He is true to his name.
>
> If I should walk in the valley of darkness
> No Evil would I fear.
> You are there with your crook and your
> staff;
> With these you give me comfort.
>
> *(Sister Bernard as usual joins in the chant
> when the last two lines are repeated.)*

You are there with your crook and your
staff;
With these you give me comfort.

Sister Bernard (*Getting up and beginning to walk* about
her cell again.)

My favourite psalm. We always sing it
before we go out to work in the gardens.
I'm no gardener mind you.
I don't know the difference between a
geranium and a chry-santhe…
Chry-santhe-mum.

But I do remember, so many years ago
now, the bog cotton swaying in the breeze
in the Wicklow Mountains. And, onetime,
the wild orchids in central Crete.
God's *al fresco* art.

We Cistercians, you know, take a vow of
stability.
So now I'm a Calder stabile in God's *hortus
conclusus*.
A motionless heron on the same rock in the
same stream.

Working in the garden near the stone wall
of the perimeter, I sometimes hear the
sound of a car.
Or a plane overhead.
People going somewhere.

(Now with some air of rejoicing.)

My real joy is the kitchen garden.
Digging, weeding, raking, planting.
Giving my limbs a work-out. Getting down
to it.
And when a robin comes looking for
worms after I've turned the earth, an
epiphany.

And I can see why the ancient Greeks
thought of the sun as divine, and the rain a
nymph.
They're the givers of light, warmth,
moisture... growth.
The ancients believed the gods themselves,
Zeus and all the rest, were the offspring of
Mother Earth, Gaia.
Yes, Mother Earth, not Father Earth.

It makes sense. If you add rain and sun, there's not much more you need than good soil.

Though the ancient Greeks knew that the gods of earth, air, fire and water could turn against you at any moment.

*(Pause, **sits down for a moment on the edge of her bed.**)*

I must admit there's one bit of gardening I really really like.

Cutting the hedge, with the petrol-powered clippers.

After weeks of silence, a jam session!

*(Sister Bernard now suddenly **gets up again and begins doing vigorous exercises** involving flinging her arms and legs about in various un-nunlike ways. She speaks **breathlessly** as she exercises.)*

If I don't exercise… I get… piles… headaches… bad breath… bad temper… I'll do something… desperate.

Again.

*(Then her **exercises suddenly turn into a
dance rhythm** from the sixties, and she
sings.)*

We're gonna rock around the clock tonight,
We're gonna rock, rock, rock, 'till broad
daylight,
We're gonna rock, gonna rock around
around... the clock...tonight

*(Her voice trails off as she **stops both
singing and dancing** and **sits down again
on the edge of the bed**. Then wistfully.)*

In those days America was technicolour
dreamland.

It's OK. Sister Patrick wouldn't have heard
me. She's as deaf as a politician who's just
been re-elected.

*(She then **smells her habit**, now sweaty
after her exercises and dancing.)*

Yuck! Smelly.

*(**Picking up the scapular** of her habit and
looking at it.)*

Same drab clothing everyday. Though it doesn't always smell as bad as this.
Washed just once a week.

(Sniffs the scapular.)

No perfume allowed, of course.

(Looking down at her shoes.)

Good sensible shoes. No Louboutins or Jimmy Choo.
My mother would have approved.

(Gets up and starts her polar bear pacing.)

How I loved clothes. Fashion. The Sixties.

They usually talk about the Sixties in terms of The Beatles and The Stones and Warhol... And Bill Haley of course.
I saw him once. And his Rockets. Live.
But they're males one and all.
When you think about it, the Sixties was really a women's movement.
We were the performance artists of the high street, and sometimes of the low streets as well.

Twiggy, Shrimpton… Tree… yeah,
Penelope Tree. Loved the name.
And Mary Quant, of course.

Womens' clothes became colourful.
Primary colours. Dashing. Affordable.

We were mad for prints – geometric prints,
stripes and dots, splashes and spots.
And we were mad for pants.
We commandeered them.
Hot pants, tight pants, skinny pants, flared
pants, patterned pants… ditched our
dresses and panted for pants.

Then there were mini-skirts, go-go boots,
plastic boots, culottes. And no stockings
or suspender belts or corsets.
Just pull on your tights and away you go.
Ready for the new day.

We were the avant-garde, out in front,
facing the barrage.
Though the barrage was often just pervy
paparazzi and leering labourers.

Well at least I don't have to worry any more about shaving my legs or my armpits, or anywhere else.

(Still pacing about, but now breaking into song.)

Hairy Mary, quite contrary,
How does your garden grow?

(Pulling herself up short, she stops and goes over to the prie-dieu and kneels.)

OK, OK, Okaaay… I know. I know.
God, I'm sorry.
Sorreee.
I've yet to die to the past.

Another trip to Fr Benedict, I guess.
More monastic medicine.
Exiled into the Valley of Wormwood.

(With a chuckle.)

Or Wormwood Scrubs.

I admit my spiritual life is no sweet cultivated garden.

It's *garigue* – dry scrubland with rocky outcrops and thorny spurge.

*(Now **gets up from the prie dieu** and just stands there.)*

Why this... this aridity? Acidie. Acid in my soul.
Old worn-out-battery acid.

After all I've been gifted with a simple, regulated life.
Fed and clothed, gratis, for more than thirty years.
So why this... this ingratitude?

Is it that rule and ritual kill individuality?
Originality?
Kill the *me* in me?

That's what St Benedict intended, of course, so that I'd give myself to another.
To God.
That's why they take away your name and give you a new one, a holy one.
And that's why they take away your clothes and give you a uni-form of black and

white, a uni-shape.

Yet what joy I had at Taking the Veil.

Being admitted to this ancient order.

So, I guess, my kicking against the pricks is

really just a refusal to submit to

St Benedict's square-bashing.

SEXT

It is now twelve noon, and **Sister Bernard is dressed and again seated at her table writing in her diary.** *The abbey* **bell sounds** *calling the nuns to chant their Sext prayers – namely for the second of the three "hours" whose psalms and antiphons commemorate the Passion of Christ and are proffered as aids to resist temptation.*

At the sound of the bell, Sister Bernard gets up from her table *and once again* **kneels at the prie-dieu,** *at the left-hand side of the stage, facing the audience, and awaits the chanting of Psalm 107.*

Chorus of Nuns   *(Chanting.)*

Some were sick on account of their sins

And afflicted on account of their guilt.

They had loathing for every food;

They came close to the gates of death.

Then they cried to the Lord in their need
And he rescued them from their distress.
He sent forth his word to heal them
And saved their life from the grave.

Let them thank the Lord for his love,
For the wonders he does for his people.
Let them offer a sacrifice of thanks
And tell of his deeds with rejoicing.

*(Sister Bernard as usual joins in the chant
when the last two lines are repeated.)*

Let them offer a sacrifice of thanks
And tell of his deeds with rejoicing.

Sister Bernard *(Getting up from the prie-dieu and
walking slowly around the cell.)*

Sacrifice. It was something the ancient
gods always demanded.
Submission.
Propitiation.
Worship.
Our Christian God's no different.

To sacrifice correctly you had to give

up something that was precious. Then
ritually destroy it. Immolate it.

At Lent, as a child, I'd give up the iced
cakes Nana made and gave me whenever I
did her shopping.
She'd say, "That's something nice for you
for doing an old lady's shopping."
And in Lent she'd add, "God would want
you to have it".
But I'd refuse.
I was very devout.
But I didn't go on to smash her cakes.
I loved Nana.

What am I to give up now?
Self. Embrace self-denial.
The world. Incarnate my denial to the
world.

As a child, when told about "enclosed
nuns" like the Carmelites and Cistercians,
I found it frightening.
Sinister.
Locking up girls behind walls and grilles.
Before they'd lived.

Once I was taken by my mother to a
Carmelite convent where a relative of
hers was being enclosed. The grille had
spikes on it, facing outward.
Perhaps every now and again they'd find
a distraught lover or adoring father, robbed
of his darling daughter, impaled on the
spikes.

Such a strange thing, sacrifice.
It's not as if *any god* needed *anything*.
It's we who need a god of some sort.
Someone to look up to.
Something better.

But does it really matter if there's someone
up there or not?
Or *anything* at all?
Perhaps all we need is an *idea* of a God.
An ideal.
The Resurrection and Ascension just extras?
Tassels?

Perhaps our sense of the sacred's been
inherited now by great works of art,
especially great music.

We come to them in holy hush.

They represent humans at their most creative.

Humans at their best.

To be set against the world's all too pervasive sights of humans at their worst.

I'd better stop or by bedtime I'll be a heretic and ready to be immolated like Giordano Bruno.

(*After a moment in silence she **gets up and starts pacing** round the cell.*)

Polar bear time again.

(*Then, after pacing in silence, **the door of her cell is opened a little and a small plate of food, a fork, a piece of bread and a glass of water are pushed around the door.** Sister Bernard goes and **picks of the plate, bread, fork and glass and sits at her table.** She **takes a mouthful.***)

Sext. Noon. Half-time, orange time.

(***Sniffs** the food.*)

It's spaghetti in onion water.
An abbey regular.

*(Another **couple of mouthfuls**.)*

No parmesan. No ciabatta. No vino.
Not even a glass of Lacrima Christi?
That's a sin!

*(After **another couple of mouthfuls**.)*

But, dear Lord, I'm famished.

*(Another **mouthful**.)*

I'd like to point out to Reverend Mother
the Church's star turn, San Tommaso
d'Aquino, dear old St Thomas Aquinas,
was no match-stick.
He didn't get his paunch on spaghetti in
onion water.

*(After taking the **last couple of mouthfuls**.)*

OK, I admit it. I've never been good at
"mortification of the flesh".
Even the phrase sounds sinister. One is to
mortify, *rendi morto*, make dead "the

flesh". As if it were a parasite on the human person.
To be surgically removed.

But without the flesh there'd be no emotions.
No grief, no tears, no love with its sweet and-sour heart.

Diary time.

*(She **sits at her desk. Belches**.)*

Oops. Sorry.

*(She **begins to write**.)*

The twin to "mortification of the flesh" is "custody of the eyes".
A nun's not supposed to look at pictures of naked men, or presumably women either.
Especially at those Speedo ads of long ago, for men 's swimming costumes.

*(Chuckles, still in **Voice Over**.)*

Embryo costumes.

I'm not allowed even to glance *deliberately*

at, say, the young Polish priest's bum.
In this forum, the eyes don't have it.

This diary is not going well at all. It seems
to be going downhill, at an ever faster rate.

I've even written 'dairy' instead of 'diary'.
Dairy.
Nuns in black and white habits grazing in
the garden.
Friesian cows.
Freudian cows.

NONES

It is now 3.00 p.m., and **Sister Bernard is dressed and seated
at her table writing in her diary.** *The abbey bell sounds
calling the nuns to chant their Nones prayers – namely for
the third of the three "hours" whose psalms and antiphons
commemorate the hour of Christ's crucifixion but also, at
Nones, the coming of the Holy Spirit, and so they are also
proffered as an aid to repentance and renewal of grace.*

At the sound of the bell, **Sister Bernard stands up, moves
away from her table** *and once again* **kneels at the prie-dieu,**
*at the left hand side of the stage, facing the audience, and
awaits the chanting of Psalm 127.*

Chorus of Nuns *(Chanting.)*

If the Lord does not build the house,
In vain do its builders labour;
If the Lord does not watch over the city,
In vain do the watchers keep vigil.

In vain is your early rising,
Your going later to rest,
You who toil for the bread you eat,
When he pours gifts on his beloved
while they slumber.

Yes, children are a gift from the Lord,
A blessing, the fruit of the womb.
The sons and daughters of youth
Are like arrows in the hand of a warrior.

*(Sister Bernard as usual **joins in the chant**
when the last two lines are repeated.)*

The sons and daughters of youth
Are like arrows in the hand of a warrior.

Sister Bernard *(**Getting up and beginning to walk** about
her cell again.)*
Well, nun's quivers are empty.

Unlike my Mum's. She had six arrows and
would have been in line for a Papal
Mutterkreuz first class.
Not all of her arrows hit targets, mind you.
But when I eventually entered the convent,
she was in holy ecstasy, as if she'd been
canonised.
And I was her gift to God.

Now if only the church would allow
cloning, they'd have no problem with
vocations.
They'd have labs full of Hildegard's just
waiting to plug the gaps.

(Stops and chants again in a quieter voice.)

The sons and daughters of youth
Are like arrows in the hand of a warrior.

(Begins to pace up and down her cell.)

The chanting. The sacred chanting.
Our *a cappella* tribal rhythm of
supplication and repentance.
Music.
God's universal notation.

With Bach his favourite note-taker.

I fear I secretly worship Apollo.
Wasn't half good-looking either, was he?
Imagine him in Speedos!

(*Stops walking. After a pause.*)

I should be working in the kitchen now or
cleaning the toilets.
Out and about anyway.

(**Begins pacing** *again.*)

Polar bear time again.
My mind's just going blank.
Blankety blank.
No holy thoughts. No unholy thoughts.
No thoughts.
No. No. Nooo. Nothing. *Niente. Nichts.*
Nada.
When it should be Yes, Yes, Yeeees.

(*Stops pacing.*)

Soon I'll be joining Sister Dalmatia in the
cloister for cloudy minds.

(Begins pacing again.)

I'd like to take a nap now, but I mustn't.
Nones is the hour of Christ's death.

(Goes to the table, opens her diary and begins to write.)

Oh Lord, cure my unbelief.
Bring belief. Relief.

A philosopher's belief is no help. Holding
to some viewpoint on the basis of
favourable probabilities.
To be honest, God, you don't do well in the
probabilities stakes.
Then the philosophers tried to find You with
the natural law that "Everything must have
a cause". But found themselves
embarrassed when they ended up with You
as an Uncaused Cause.

Belief needs a jet engine, with an after
burner.
Not a course in logic or scientific method.
It needs need, desire.
Kierkegaard's "leap of faith".

I like that.

Though it seems a bit too energetic for
poor Søren, limping around his beloved
Frederiksberg Gardens with his cane and
top-hat.

Leaping reminds me of the long jump at
school, in my navy-blue bloomers.
If you wobble in your run-up, because of
some doubt, you'll miss stepping on the
wooden plank just before the sand pit, and
be disqualified.
And then, if it happened a lot, you'd be
told to try the javelin.

I suspect Kierkegaard meant faith's not an
intellectual exercise.
Not a matter of theology, natural or
unnatural.
But a passionate "yes" whose utterance
alone annihilates all doubts, all
uncertainties, and all curiosity.
Belief is YES made flesh.

You must leap! Leap *out of* faith. *In* faith
On faith.

(Gets up, and wanders distractedly around the cell.)

So I must learn again to leap. But *learn* doesn't seem right.

Besides shouldn't *love* come into it somewhere?
Aren't we supposed to *love* God, not just believe in Him?
Yet there's something odd about my saying contritely,
"Dear God, when was the last time I said I loved you?"

Fearful worship and needy prayers seem more natural.
As they were for the ancient Greeks.

Help me! Heeeeelp!

*(**Stops walking** about and **begins to sing** "Amazing Grace".)*

Amazing grace! How sweet the sound,
That saved a wretch; like me!

*(At this point the **Chorus of Nuns joins in.**)*

I once was lost, but now am found,
Was blind, but now I see.

*(Then glancing at the prie-dieu, she goes to it and **kneels down**.)*

VESPERS

*It is now 6.00 p.m., and **Sister Bernard is dressed and seated on the edge of her bed.** The abbey bell sounds calling the nuns to chant Vespers – whose psalms and antiphons praise the Lord at the end of the convent's working day.*

***At the sound of the bell, Sister Bernard stands up, moves away from the bed** and once again **kneels at the prie-dieu,** at the left-hand side of the stage, facing the audience, and awaits the chanting of Psalm 148.*

Chorus of Nuns   *(Chanting.)*

Allelujia!
Praise the Lord from the heavens,
Praise him in the heights.
Praise him, all his angels,
Praise him, all his host.

Praise him, sun and moon,
Praise him, shining stars.
Praise him, highest heavens

And the waters above the heavens.

Let them praise the name of the Lord
For he alone is exalted.
The splendor of his name
Reaches beyond heaven and earth.
Alleluia!

*(Sister Bernard as usual joins in the chant
when the last few lines are repeated.)*

The splendor of his name
Reaches beyond heaven and earth.
Alleluia!

*(Getting up from the prie-dieu and
walking about.)*

Well, Alleluia indeed. The end of another
day.
Well almost. Vespers.
Hallelujah!
Praise the Lord!

We're often told to *Carpe diem*! "Seize the
day!"
But everyone forgets the rest of what

Horace said,

quam minimum credula postero,

"trusting as little as possible in the future".

I'm not sure what "carpe-ing" of the day I
did today.
I mean, what can I do here in my cell the
whole time?

But I've done lots of carping, I fear.
And lots of not trusting in anything very
much.
Shadow boxing with myself about
everything.
I'll have to tell Fr Benedict I was crapulous
all day.

*(At this point her supper of **a piece of
bread and glass of water** is passed around
her cell door. She **sits down** with the food.)*

Let them eat bread.

*(After a **munch or two**.)*

This bread's not half bad.
Sister Ursula in the bakery gets better and

better.

She'll need to watch it or she'll get solitary.

Or be told to put more sour into the sour dough.

*(**Picks up one of the books** on the table. Ruminating.)*

Reverend Mother gave me four books for my incarceration.

One of them – Hint! Hint! I suspect – was this, "The Rule of St Benedict".

That's the rule for our conventual life.

Now the very last chapter, Caput 73 of The Rule, says

"This Rule is only a beginning of perfection".

Perfection! Sweet Jesus!

Sorry! But that's not wandering about in the holy foothills, is it?

Our monastic life, it says, provides us with the "tools for the cultivation of virtues", including their "loftier summits", thereby to "hasten towards our heavenly home",

the pinnacle of our existence.
Holy crampons provided.

So we're here to be not just holy, but
perfectly holy.
Full of the virtues at their loftiest level, as
passports into heaven.
No need to queue.

Now, *this* does puzzle me. How can I be
virtuous locked away in a silent enclosure?
Is religious perfection something
completely different from being moral?
Just a matter of having no imperfections?
Being immaculate?
No everyday shit on your shoes?

Put it this way, how could I be moral all by
myself on a holy island?
For Robinson Crusoe on his tropical island
the moral life began, whether he liked it or
not, when Man Friday showed up and
cramped his style.
He suddenly had to think about someone
other than himself. About the effect of his
actions on another person. About sharing.

He had to fight against his ego.

How can I be moral all by myself in an
enclosed convent?

Missing the point, St Benedict would reply,
I suspect.
The monastic life is designed to be "out of
this world".
It's a life looking always *upwards*, away
from Earth, to God.
Like Sister Teresa does.

But then God can always look *downwards*
and command that we kill Isaac.
How does that fit in?

*(Then glancing at the prie dieu, she goes to
it and* **kneels down.***)*

Sister Teresa pray for me.
Help me in my unbelief.

COMPLINE

It is now 9.00 p.m., and **Sister Bernard is dressed and seated
on the edge of her bed. The abbey bell sounds** *calling the
nuns to chant Compline – whose psalms and antiphons praise*

*the Lord and urge the nuns to think of "the last things"
(death, judgment, hell and heaven). For this is the last
liturgical hour of the day and now the nuns are to go to bed
soon afterwards in order to snatch some sleep before they rise
again for Vigils.*

At the sound of the bell, Sister Bernard, *who has been sitting
at her table,* **stands up** *once again,* **kneels at the prie dieu**
*at the left-hand side of the stage, facing the audience, and
awaits the chanting of Psalm 143.*

Sister Bernard　　*(After kneeling she **gets up** momentarily
and **rubs her right knee.**)*

I have Bernadines' bursitis.
None of us escapes in the end.
Fr Benedict said I should just "offer it up".
As a sacrifice.

*(Then she **returns to kneeling at the prie
dieu.**)*

Chorus of Nuns　　*(Chanting.)*

I remember the days that are past;
I ponder all your works.
I muse on what your hand has wrought
And to you I stretch out my hands.
Like a parched land my soul thirsts for you.

Lord, make haste and answer;
For my spirit fails within me.
Do not hide your face
Lest I become like those in the grave.

In the morning let me know your love
For I put my trust in you.
Make me know the way I should walk;
To you I lift up my soul.

*(Sister Bernard as usual joins in the chant
when the last few lines are repeated.)*

Make me know the way I should walk;
To you I lift up my soul.

Sister Bernard *(**Getting up from the prie dieu and
going over to the bed** she takes out her
plain white cotton nightdress from under
the pillow and **starts to undress and put on
her nightdress**.)*

Compline. The completion of the monastic
day.
The end of the day.
Then the only end of days.

Will *my* end be like the ancient Greeks thought?

Those whom the gods mark for death they first drive mad. Like poor Sister Dalmatia.

Or will I be one of those whom the gods mark for death by first making them so sick that they want to die?

Like poor old Sister Gertrude.

She was in such pain from cancer of the spine, that you could hear the screams from the infirmary.

Dying for death.

*(She **finishes undressing and putting on her nightdress.**)*

If death really is the necessary bus ticket to the next better world, perhaps cancer doesn't seem quite so unfair.

It's just the bus arriving a bit early and crushing your legs at the same time.

But what if death is the terminus?

*(She **stands up and then wanders around her cell.**)*

After the age of sixty-five perhaps everyone becomes an Existentialist? Being. And then *Nothingness?*

The butterflies and flowers in the convent garden briefly shimmy and shine, then die.
Even our sun will become extinct.
Why should we humans be the one exception to this law of nature?
Classical Judaism always accepted death as the end.
The dead end.
With nobility, or at least resignation.
Why are Christians such bad losers?

Perhaps it's insulting to God to *want* more.
As if the gift of life were not enough.

*(**Staring up through the skylight** at the moon.)*

I used to love the moon.
Partly support for the underdog, as we've always given the moon such a bad press.
Prone to turning people into lunatics, or werewolves, our ancestors were told.

But everything looks softer in moonlight.
God's candlelight, to light our way home
after our struggles in the glare of day.
As the sun goes down there's that change of
palette from sun-bleached blue to
cornflower blue to Prussian blue.
God taught Titian.

But then some American tourists landed on
the moon and took some photos.
And it's never been the same since.

(Stopping by her bed)

I'm meant now to go to bed after a final
prayer and holy thought. St Hildegard
would thank God for all the graces He'd
given her that day.
And thank Him for a vision or two.

*(Then **walks on** again.)*

The only visions I'm likely to have before
bedtime are of my mother carrying a plate
of roast lamb, Brussells sprouts and roast
potatoes to the dinner table.
And gravy. Thick axle-grease gravy.

Ah, those now fast-fading faces of
childhood delight and innocent greed.

(Pause.)

To be frank I'm not much taken by the
thought of a life after death with Hildegard
and Sister Theresa and all the other saints.
No Bill Haley there.

When death comes, if it's an option, I'll
probably be only too happy to call it a day.

Earth to earth, ashes to ashes, dust to dust.
That sounds right and proper.
A humble surrender to Gaia and gravity.

Mind you, they give you a grand send-off
here, in the convent.

The last one was for Sister Gertrude.
As you lie in your coffin in the chapel, they
lay a crown of thorns on your corpse.
A symbol of your sacrificial life.
And all the nuns keep a vigil throughout
the night.
Awake but not a wake.

The coffin's a plain wooden box. Pine.
No brass or varnish.
Made in our own workshop.

Sister Gertrude would have been
disappointed with the eulogy she got from
Fr Benedict, but then she wasn't around to
hear it.
He has a sort of template into which he just
places the name of the latest nun to die.
A sort of sibilant show. As on each
occasion he declares the dead nun's life to
have been one of service, sacrifice and
sanctity, using exactly the same words for
every nun he buries.

Then, as they carry you out after the
requiem mass, the whole community chants
the *De Profundis*.
No, not Wilde's, the psalm.
And, of course, you're buried within the
convent's grounds, just behind the chapel.
With only your nun's name on the little
cross.

*(She **gets up, goes over to the bed and***

extracts the chamber-pot from underneath
it, and sits on it.)

The hours.
Then the only end of hours.

I still have the irreverent dream of waking
up one morning with no schedule.
Being able to get up at any hour of the day,
and wander around all day in pyjamas,
with nothing in particular to do?
Satin pyjamas. Scarlet ones!
Heaven!

*(While she's still **sitting on the chamber-***
***pot**, there's a **knock at the cell door**.)*

Come in!

Reverend   *(Entering and, seeing Sister Bernard on*
Mother   *the pot, looks away, a bit embarrassed.)*

Ah, I see.
Not the best moment.

Just the briefest of words then.
I hope, Sister Bernard, you've reflected on
your fall from grace

and that it was temporary.

At any rate I've decided to end your
isolation from the community.

You may join us for Vigils at midnight.

*(She **turns towards the door but then
turns back**.)*

You should come to my office after Lauds
and give me your spiritual diary.

*(**Reverend Mother closes the cell door as
she leaves. Sister Bernard arises from the
pot, adjusts her nightdress.**)*

Sister Bernard *(**Standing** in front of her bed.)*

Reverend Mother arriving while I was still
making my deposit, reminds me of
childhood.

When my father arrived home from work,
my mother would sometimes announce,
joyously, as if awarding me the laurels
of the *Victor Ludorum*, that "Daisy did
wee wees and poo in her potty all day", as
distinct from on the carpet or the kitchen
floor.

Yes, Daisy was the name I was given at birth.

From a song that my Mum and Dad liked, particularly my Dad.

The parish priest was definitely not happy.

No St Daisy in the church's list of saints.

Why does bedtime, more than anything else, remind us of childhood?

Perhaps because it was that precious time when we were read a story, tucked in and kissed good night?

Those unconditional signs of love, no matter what we'd done during the day?

(Kneeling down beside her bed, with her elbows resting on the bed, as she did in childhood when saying her bedtime prayers.)

O Lord, God the Father, please tuck me in.

(With increasing loudness.)

I ought to believe.

I must believe.

I can't believe.

I belieeeve.

(Now quietly.)

Good God, Goodnight!

Sister Bernard rises from her kneeling position and gets briefly into bed.

Then, for the first time, the Chorus of Nuns moves out of the shadows backstage and moves to the front of the stage.

Sister Bernard gets out of bed and joins them. Together they sing the Canticle of Simeon, Nunc Dimittis.

> Lord, now lettest Thou Thy servant
> depart in peace
> according to Thy Word,
> For mine eyes have seen Thy salvation
> which Thou hast prepared
> before the face of all people.
> To be a Light to light on the Gentiles
> and to be the glory
> of Thy people Israel.
> Glory be to the Father
> and to the Son
> and to the Holy Ghost,
> As it was in the beginning,
> is now and ever shall be,
> world without end.
> Amen.